Wild and Woolly
CASHMERE GOATS

Sadie Woods

New York

Published in 2018 by The Rosen Publishing Group, Inc.
29 East 21st Street, New York, NY 10010

First Edition

Editor: Theresa Morlock
Book Design: Rachel Rising

Photo Credits: Cover Daniela Duncan/Moment/Getty Images; Cover (background) SUJITRA CHAOWDEE/Shutterstock.com; Cover, pp. 1, 3, 4, 6, 8, 10, 12, 14, 16, 18, 20, 22, 23, 24 (texture) Apples Eyes Studio/Shutterstock.com; p. 5 TOMO/Shutterstock.com; p. 7 (Nubian) Dagmar Hijmans/Shutterstock.com; p. 7 (pygmy) CEW/Shutterstock.com; p. 7 (Boer) Werner Rebel/Shutterstock.com; p. 8 worldswildlifewonders/Shutterstock.com; p. 9 Perfect Lazybones/Shutterstock.com; p. 10 iStockphoto.com/Guenter Guni; p. 11 Lyubov_Nazarova/Shutterstock.com; p. 12 iStockphoto.com/Antagain; p. 13 Jag_cz/Shutterstock.com; p. 14 Vera Taraniuk/Shutterstock.com; p.15 GrapeImages/E+/Getty Images; p. 16 K PRABHU/Shutterstock.com; pp. 17, 21 Bloomberg/Bloomberg/Getty Images; p. 19 michel Setboun/Corbis Historical/Getty Images; p. 20 Vittavat Apiromsene/Shutterstock.com; p. 22 Attila Simon/Shutterstock.com.

Cataloging-in-Publication Data

Names: Woods, Sadie.
Title: Cashmere goats / Sadie Woods.
Description: New York : PowerKids Press, 2018. | Series: Wild and woolly | Includes index.
Identifiers: ISBN 9781538325995 (pbk.) | ISBN 9781538325292 (library bound) | ISBN 9781538326008 (6 pack)
Subjects: LCSH: Goats–Juvenile literature.
Classification: LCC SF383.35 W66 2018 | DDC 636.3'9–dc23

Manufactured in the United States of America

CPSIA Compliance Information: Batch #BW18PK: For Further Information contact Rosen Publishing, New York, New York at 1-800-237-9932

CONTENTS

Softer than Soft

Have you ever worn or touched a cashmere sweater? Cashmere is one of the softest **materials** in the world. Believe it or not, that cashmere originally grew on a goat! Cashmere comes from the supersoft undercoat of goats. This undercoat is removed, spun into yarn, and woven to make **velvety** cashmere clothing.

Goats are friendly, sturdy creatures. They were some of the first animals to be **domesticated** by people. Raising Cashmere goats has just begun to grow in popularity in the United States.

Fuzzy Features

One goat produces as much as 2.5 pounds (1.1 kg) of **fleece** per year. Only a small part of this fleece is cashmere.

Goats aren't only useful—
they're adorable, too!

5

A Type, Not a Breed

Cashmere goats aren't an actual goat **breed**. The name "Cashmere goat" can be used to describe any goat that produces cashmere wool. Today, most Cashmere goats are the **descendants** of meat and dairy goats that were bred because of the high amount of cashmere fiber, or hair, they produced.

A micron is a unit by which hair or fiber is measured. Cashmere fiber must be 19 microns or smaller. That's very thin compared with human hair and other animal fibers.

Fuzzy Features

There are more than 200 goat breeds in the world.

Boer goat

These are a few of the many goat breeds.

Nubian goat

pygmy goat

7

Goat Basics

Goats are happiest living in herds, or groups. Goat herds usually have a female leader called a herd queen. A male goat is called a buck or a billy. A female goat is called a doe or a nanny. Just like young people, young goats are called kids!

Kids can stand as soon as they're born and are able to walk within a few minutes of being born. Every goat has its own call and scent. Mothers use their kids' scents to find them.

⬅ **goat beard**

Fuzzy Features

Both male and female goats can have horns and beards.

Most goat kids are twins. Mother goats usually have two babies at a time.

9

Goats reach adulthood when they're about a year old. On average, they live for about 12 years. Some live even longer. You can tell how old a goat is by looking at its teeth.

Depending on their breed, goats can weigh anywhere from 22 pounds (10 kg) to 350 pounds (158.8 kg). They measure between 17 and 42 inches (43.2 cm and 106.7 cm) tall at the shoulder.

Goats can be white, black, tan, brown, or many combinations of these colors.

The sound a goat makes is called a bleat.

11

Picky Eaters

Goats are herbivores. That means they only eat plants. Some people believe goats will eat just about anything, but this is untrue. In fact, goats are somewhat picky eaters. They enjoy leaves, sticks, stems, and grass.

Goats are ruminants, which are animals that process their food in two steps. They chew their food, swallow it, spit it back up, and chew it again. Goats have a stomach with four parts called chambers. This helps them break down their food.

Goats have rectangular **pupils** in eyes that can turn. This helps them keep an eye out for predators when they're grazing.

13

A Long Partnership

Goats were some of the very first animals to be domesticated by humans. Goats are often friendly and easy to keep.

Goats may have been the first animals people kept for milk. Goatskin was once used to make parchment, or paper, to write on and bottles to carry liquids. Today, people continue to keep goats for their milk, meat, and wool. Goats have also been used to pull carts and carry packs. Some goats can carry 30 percent of their body weight.

goat dairy products ➡️

Fuzzy Features

The Egyptian pharaoh Cephranes was buried with more than 2,000 goats.

Goats can be very friendly. Most like being petted and played with.

15

Wool of Kings

Cashmere is sometimes called the "golden fleece." Historically, cashmere was the cloth preferred by royalty and wealthy people. The earliest recorded use of cashmere took place back in the 14th century!

During the 1700s, cashmere **shawls** became popular in Britain and France. Empress Josephine of France was believed to own hundreds of cashmere shawls.

Today, cashmere is still in high **demand**. Most of the world's cashmere is produced in China, Afghanistan, Iran, and India. Cashmere wool is sometimes called pashmina.

Cashmere goats are named for the Kashmir region in Asia, where cashmere shawls were historically traded.

Shearing

Cashmere goats can be sheared once a year. Shearing is the process by which fiber is collected from an animal using large scissors called shears. This is usually done during the late winter or early spring. Goats must be clean and dry before the shearing process begins. The goat must be held in place to avoid harm.

Some farmers may choose to comb or pluck the fiber from their goats rather than shear them. They remove the soft cashmere fiber slowly by hand.

Fuzzy Features

Angora goats produce a fiber called mohair. Cashmere can come from almost any non-Angora goat.

In this photo, a farmer shears a goat in Hakhorin, Mongolia.

19

Processing

Since only a very small amount of the fiber produced by a goat is considered cashmere, cashmere goat farmers spend a lot of time sorting the fiber. Removing the guard hair, or outer hair, from the softer fibers is called dehairing.

The longest, thinnest pieces of fiber are used for knitted cloth. The shorter fibers are used for woven cloth. The guard hairs can be used for rugs.

After it's sorted and cleaned, fiber can be spun. Spinning is the process by which fiber is made into yarn.

Large-scale fiber processing is often done on machines. However, many people spin their fiber at home.

Beautiful Cashmere

It takes a lot of time, care, and skill to create cashmere products. It usually takes a year for a goat to produce enough cashmere to make a single shawl!

When cashmere shawls arrived in Europe during the 18th century, people called them "ring shawls" because the fabric was so fine it could pass through the middle of a ring. Since the beginning of its use during the 1300s, cashmere has been highly prized. Each year, the demand for cashmere continues to grow.

GLOSSARY

breed: A group of animals that share features different from other groups of the kind. Also, to bring animals together to make babies.

demand: A strong request for something.

descendant: A creature that's related to a group of creatures that lived in an earlier time.

domesticate: To breed and raise animals for use by people.

fleece: The woolen coat of a sheep or goat.

material: Something from which something else can be made.

pupil: The opening in an eye that changes size to let light into the eye.

shawl: A piece of fabric worn over the shoulders or head.

velvety: Soft and fuzzy.

INDEX

WEBSITES

Due to the changing nature of Internet links, PowerKids Press has developed an
online list of websites related to the subject of this book. This site is updated regularly.
Please use this link to access the list: www.powerkidslinks.com/wandw/cashmere